WALRUSES

LIVING WILD

Published by Creative Education
P.O. Box 227, Mankato, Minnesota 56002
Creative Education is an imprint of The Creative Company
www.thecreativecompany.us

Design and production by Mary Herrmann
Art direction by Rita Marshall
Printed in the United States of America

Photographs by Alamy (Danita Delimont, F1online digitale Bildagentur GmbH, Mary Evans Picture Library, louise murray, Tsuneo Nakamura/Volvox Inc, WorldFoto), Dreamstime (Michele Cornelius, Par Edlund, Irina Gracheva, Anthony Hathaway, Michael Ludwig, Outdoorsman, Remcorutten, Vladimir Seliverstov, Twildlife), Getty Images (Paul Souders), iStockphoto (Josef Friedhuber, John Gollop), Shutterstock (AlexanderZam, BMJ, Hal Brindley, Gail Johnson, Dominic Laniewicz, Light & Magic Photography, Alberto Loyo, Charles Masters, Vladimir Melnik, Jamen Percy, PSD photography, rook76, Howard Sandler, Wild Arctic Pictures, Elena Yakusheva), SuperStock (Minden Pictures, NaturePL, Prisma), U.S. Geological Survey (Department of the Interior/USGS), Wikipedia (Captain Budd Christman/NOAA Corps, Floyd Davidson, Albrecht Durer, Hbobrien)

Library of Congress Cataloging-in-Publication Data
Gish, Melissa.
Walruses / by Melissa Gish.
p. cm. — (Living wild)
Includes index.
Summary: A look at walruses, including their habitats, physical characteristics such as their lengthy tusks, behaviors, relationships with humans, and protected status in the world today.
ISBN 978-1-60818-291-6
1. Walrus—Juvenile literature. I. Title.

QL737.P62G57 2013
599.79'9—dc23   2012023309

First Edition
9 8 7 6 5 4 3 2 1

C CREATIVE EDUCATION

WALRUSES

Melissa Gish

It is summer in the Beaufort Sea off Alaska's northern coast, where massive ice sheets have fractured. About 40 walruses are piled together on an ice floe, basking in the sun.

It is summer in the Beaufort Sea off Alaska's northern coast, where massive ice sheets have fractured, giving way to wide swaths of bone-chilling, 29 °F (-1.7 °C) water. About 40 walruses are piled together on an ice floe, basking in the sun. One small walrus, only a few months old, croaks and cries. Panic-stricken, it has been dragging itself around the edge of the ice, peering into the dark sea for nearly an hour. Earlier, while the walruses had been

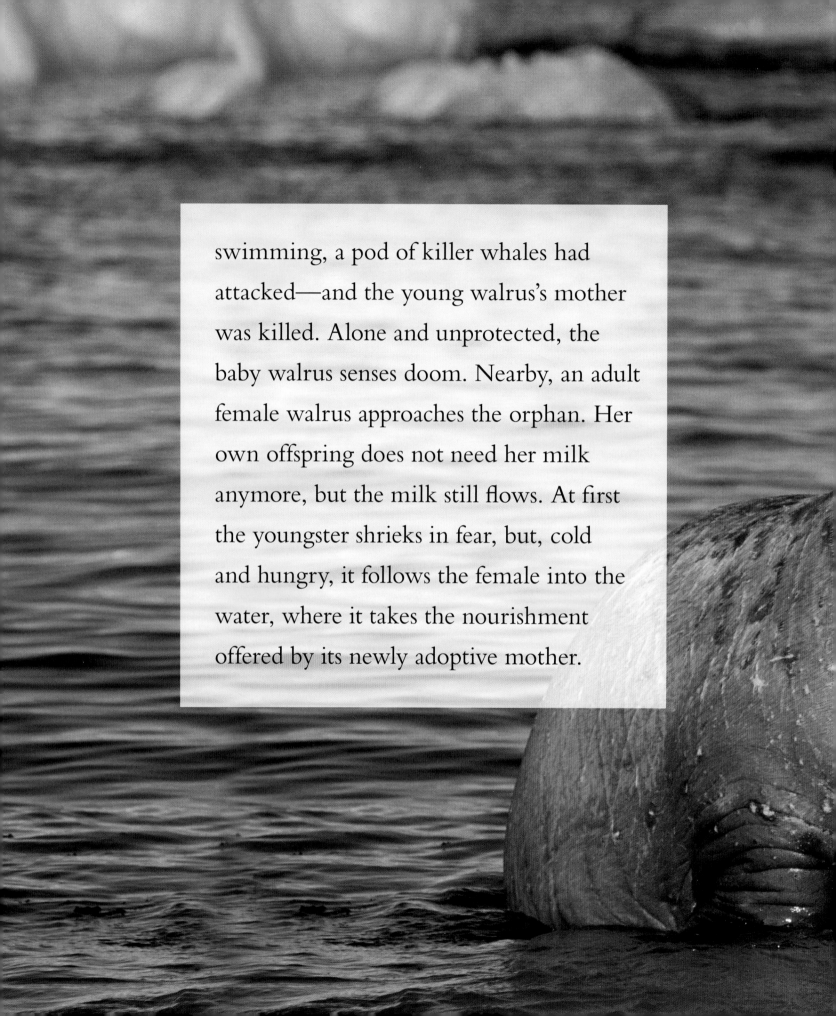

swimming, a pod of killer whales had attacked—and the young walrus's mother was killed. Alone and unprotected, the baby walrus senses doom. Nearby, an adult female walrus approaches the orphan. Her own offspring does not need her milk anymore, but the milk still flows. At first the youngster shrieks in fear, but, cold and hungry, it follows the female into the water, where it takes the nourishment offered by its newly adoptive mother.

WHERE IN THE WORLD THEY LIVE

■ **Pacific Walrus**
Bering Sea
between Alaska
and Russia

□ **Atlantic Walrus**
Nunavut, Baffin
Island, Greenland,
Labrador,
Newfoundland

■ **Laptev Walrus**
Laptev Sea

The three walrus subspecies are found in the far northern waters of the Arctic region. More than 100,000 Pacific walruses inhabit the area between Alaska and Russia, while one-fifth as many Atlantic walruses can be found in the Atlantic Ocean near Greenland and Canada. Laptev walruses are named for their native home of the Laptev Sea and number only about 10,000. The colored squares represent common locations of each subspecies.

ARCTIC GIANTS

W alruses are the only members of the Odobenidae family, which is part of the Pinnipedia group of marine **mammals**. Pinnipeds are found mostly in cold-water coastal or island habitats around the world and are characterized by their streamlined bodies and short, wide, **webbed** flippers. The word "pinniped" derives from the Latin *pinna*, meaning "wing" or "fin," and *pedis*, meaning "foot." This group of fin-footed animals includes eared seals (sea lions and fur seals) and true, or earless, seals as well as three subspecies of marine mammals with tusks—walruses—which are named for the regions in which they are found.

The most abundant subspecies is the Pacific walrus. It is found in the Bering Sea from Bristol Bay south into the Gulf of Anadyr, the Bering Strait, and the Chukchi Sea—the Arctic waters that lie between northern Alaska and Russia. About 130,000 Pacific walruses exist today. Far fewer Atlantic walruses—about 20,000—are found in the icy waters around northeastern Nunavut (a Canadian territory), Baffin Island, and Greenland, and from the Hudson Strait southward along the coasts

Aging males develop bumps, called bosses, on their skin, which turn a pale pink color.

A walrus's powerful mouth suction can draw out the flesh of a mollusk in a matter of seconds, leaving the shell unbroken.

of Labrador and Newfoundland. The third and least populous subspecies, the Laptev walrus, is found only in the Laptev Sea. Approximately 10,000 Laptev walruses live among the small islands between the Arctic Ocean and the northern coast of Siberia.

The name "walrus" is an English translation of the Danish word *hvalros* (*VALE-hoss*), meaning "sea horse." Walruses and their relatives live mostly in the water. To help insulate their organs and protect themselves against heat loss in their icy habitat, walruses have a six-inch (15.2 cm) layer of fat, called blubber, just beneath a four-inch (10.2 cm) layer of skin.

When the walrus is in the water, the blood vessels in its skin constrict, forcing blood toward the walrus's organs and reducing heat loss. When this happens, the walrus's skin appears pale—almost white—and its body is able to stay up to five degrees warmer than the water temperature. When the walrus is on land, the blood vessels in its skin expand, releasing heat into the environment, causing the walrus's skin to turn pink. If a walrus starts to get too warm on land, it will return to the water to cool off. Walruses prepare for cold winter weather by eating more food and

A walrus's front (pectoral) flippers have the same skeletal structure as the hands or front paws of other mammals.

An adult walrus typically spends two-thirds of its life in the water, traveling more easily there than on land.

building up their layer of blubber. In winter, walruses may add up to one-third more body mass.

Male walruses are called bulls, and females are called cows. The walruses in the Pacific and Laptev seas grow larger than their Atlantic cousins. Adult male Atlantic walruses weigh up to 1,700 pounds (771 kg) in summer but can bulk up to 2,800 pounds (1,270 kg) in the winter. Adult male Pacific walruses can weigh up to 2,000 pounds (907 kg) in summer and up to 3,700 pounds (1,678 kg) in winter. Females are about half the size of males. The walrus is the second-largest pinniped after the bull southern elephant seal, which can weigh 8,820 pounds (4,000 kg).

Walruses and their relatives have streamlined bodies, a shape that allows for little **resistance** as the animals cut through the water, enabling them to dive, maneuver, and surface easily. Seals and sea lions are slenderer than walruses, but walruses can navigate underwater as well as their smaller cousins can. Other than size, the main differences among the pinnipeds can be found by observing the flippers and head.

Unlike walruses, sea lions have long flippers. The front

The large proboscis, or snout, of an adult bull elephant seal resembles an elephant's trunk.

A walrus's ribcage can partially collapse to force excess air out of the lungs—important for surviving deep-sea dives.

To "walk," walruses scoot their back flippers forward, and then pull forward with their front flippers.

flippers are used for swimming and the rear flippers for steering. Earless seals and walruses move differently, using their short front flippers to steer and their rear flippers to propel their bodies through the water. On land, earless seals drag themselves or wriggle their bodies forward, but sea lions and walruses are able to bend their back flippers forward and their front flippers backward to create a set of four feet on which to walk. The bottoms of a walrus's front flippers have small claws and fleshy bumps that help the walrus grip icy surfaces as it moves.

Additionally, eared seals such as sea lions are called "eared seals" because they have small ear flaps, but earless seals and walruses have only tiny openings for their ears. The definitive feature that sets the walrus apart from all its relatives is the massive set of tusks protruding from the upper jaw. Both male and female walruses grow tusks, which are long teeth deeply embedded in their skulls. The tusks of Pacific walruses are slightly longer and more curved than those of Atlantic walruses. A male Pacific walrus's tusks may reach 40 inches (102 cm) in length, and a female's may reach 32 inches (81.3 cm). Walruses use their tusks to pull themselves onto shore or ice floes,

break through ice to make breathing holes, or scrape away the seafloor to expose clams and other food sources. Male walruses also use their tusks while fighting.

Surrounding the tusks are 400 to 700 stiff whiskers that are attached to sensitive nerves beneath the skin of

The behavior of walruses fighting each other with their tusks is called tusking.

Several of the 1,250 species of sea cucumber inhabiting the ocean floor are included in the diet of walruses.

Though walruses rarely eat carrion, they have been observed feeding on dead whales that wash up on shore.

the walrus's face. These whiskers, called vibrissae, can detect vibrations caused by prey in the water while the walrus forages. In addition to the tusks, walruses have 18 teeth that are sharply ridged for opening the shells of their prey. Walruses are carnivores, meaning they eat other animals such as fish, clams, crustaceans, and sea cucumbers—squishy, caterpillar-shaped **invertebrates** that vary in size from one inch (2.5 cm) to more than six feet (1.8 m) in length, depending on the species. Walruses typically stuff themselves on a variety of prey twice a day, foraging exclusively in the water. To keep from inhaling water when they feed, walruses have special muscles in their noses that pinch their nostrils tightly shut.

Walruses can dive as deep as 300 feet (91.4 m). Walrus muscle has a high concentration of a substance called myoglobin, which enables oxygen to be stored and helps walruses stay underwater for long periods of time—up to 25 minutes. Underwater, walruses hear as well as they do on land, but their eyesight is weaker than that of other pinnipeds. A nictitating (*NIK-tih-tayt-ing*) membrane (a see-through inner eyelid) closes over walruses' eyes to protect them from debris and sand.

Walruses' tusks start growing when they are about 8 months old but do not become visible for about 18 months.

Some scientists predict that Arctic summers will be ice-free by the 2050s, leaving walruses with little habitat.

CHILLING OUT

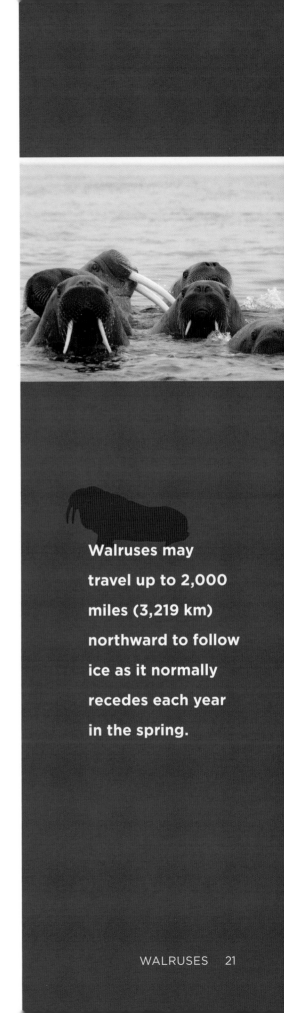

Walruses spend most of their time at sea, even sleeping while bobbing upright. A walrus has an air sac under its throat that keeps its head above the surface while the rest of the body is underwater. Walruses are social animals that communicate above water with sounds such as groans, barks, grunts, and teeth-clacking. Underwater, they whistle, and males use their air sacs to make sounds like the tolling of a bell. Walruses vocalize to establish territories, call out to family members, warn of predators, and signal food sources.

On land, a group of walruses is called a haul-out. At sea, walruses gather in groups called herds. Walrus herds, which typically contain either all males or all females and their young offspring, may number in the hundreds. During mating season, which takes place between December and March, mature walruses gather in special groups, called leks, on rocky shores or ice floes in the same locations each year in preparation for mating. Male leks are battlegrounds where the largest walruses with the longest tusks fight for the right to approach females that

Walruses may travel up to 2,000 miles (3,219 km) northward to follow ice as it normally recedes each year in the spring.

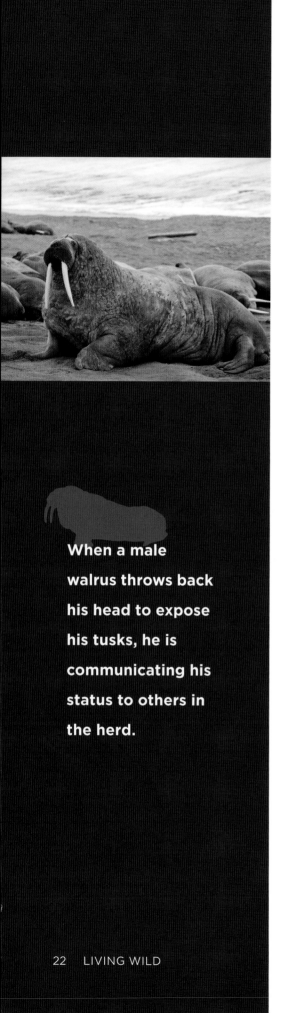

When a male walrus throws back his head to expose his tusks, he is communicating his status to others in the herd.

have gathered themselves into neighboring leks made up of mature females who are not already pregnant from the year before. Bulls will push and bite each other and stab at one another with their tusks, sometimes causing serious wounds, until one bull backs off. Male walruses may even fight to the death for dominance in a lek.

Walrus cows are old enough to mate by age 5 or 6, though they usually do not become pregnant until they are closer to 10 years old. Bulls mature by age 8 to 10, but they typically will not mate until they are older. Herds of young male walruses travel away from older bulls during mating season to avoid dangerous confrontations. By the time a bull is 15, he has the strength to become dominant in a male lek.

A dominant bull establishes a space 20 to 30 feet (6–9.1 m) away from other males, where it swims around a female lek, vocalizing to get the females' attention. Underwater, the male makes bell-like and loud knocking sounds for several minutes. When he surfaces, he whistles and rapidly chatters his jaw to make a clacking sound. When a female has become sufficiently interested in the male, she leaves the lek and enters the water with the

male, where the two engage in a courtship swim that includes nuzzling and diving together. The walruses mate underwater, after which the male leaves the female and begins vocalizing again to attract the attention of other females. One male walrus may breed with as many as 20 different females before returning to his all-male herd. He will have nothing to do with the rearing of the calves, leaving that task to the mothers of his offspring.

Walrus courtship may move from the water to ice and back again before mating takes place.

The bond between a mother walrus and her calf is the strongest among all the pinniped species.

Females typically give birth to only one calf every two to three years. For walruses, reproduction is tied to climate and food supply. A walrus's normal **gestation** is 15 to 16 months, which includes a 4- to 5-month period of delayed implantation. This means that after the female walrus's egg is fertilized, it turns into a ball of cells that floats in the female's **uterus** for a time before it develops into a baby walrus. Such a delay allows a female walrus that mates every year to finish nursing and caring for one calf before giving birth to another. This also allows each calf to be born between April and June, when the climate is best and food is abundant. It is rare for walruses to have twins, but some cases have been observed.

Born on the ice, a newborn calf is 3.3 to 4 feet (1–1.2 m) long and weighs between 90 and 140 pounds (40.8–63.5 kg). Calves begin to swim almost immediately after birth. They have short, gray fur that turns reddish-brown during the first two weeks. This first coat of fur is gradually shed and replaced with thicker, darker fur over the next four to six weeks, and the calf becomes a strong swimmer.

Because walruses are mammals, they nurse their young with milk. While a mother walrus begins to supplement her offspring's diet with small amounts of fish and other prey when the calf is around two months of age, milk remains the calf's main food source for up to two years. Some calves nurse longer if the mother does not give birth again until the following year.

To protect their young from aggressive attacks and even accidental crushing, females with calves form separate herds from females without offspring. These nursery herds may

During freezing weather, a walrus can use its head and tusks to break ice up to eight inches (20.3 cm) thick to make a breathing hole.

Global climate change affects the entire food chain, and polar bears face new challenges when hunting walruses.

contain anywhere from 20 to 200 individuals. A mother walrus is extremely protective of her calf. She may help her calf ride on her back, and, if she feels threatened, she may clutch it to her chest, holding it under her front flippers as she swims away from danger. No other pinnipeds protect their young in such a manner.

The relationship between a mother walrus and her calf is the longest lasting of all pinnipeds'—stretching from 30 months to a lifetime. If a calf is male, he will join a male herd at age five or six, but a female may remain in her mother's herd for the rest of her life. And if a calf is orphaned, it may be adopted by a female walrus and develop a strong bond with its new mother.

As fierce as mother walruses can be, they cannot protect their offspring from all the dangers on land and in the sea. Walrus calves are often targeted by polar bears, which can weigh up to 1,500 pounds (680 kg). In the water, even adult walruses are no match for killer whales. At 26 feet (7.9 m) long, a sharp-toothed killer whale can easily swallow a young walrus whole or shred an adult walrus to pieces in seconds. A fortunate walrus can live for 40 years, though most do not survive that long in the wild.

Young walruses are physically identical to their parents in every way, except for body size.

FROM "THE WALRUS AND THE CARPENTER"

The sea was wet as wet could be,

The sands were dry as dry.

You could not see a cloud, because

No cloud was in the sky:

No birds were flying overhead—

There were no birds to fly.

The Walrus and the Carpenter

Were walking close at hand:

They wept like anything to see

Such quantities of sand:

"If this were only cleared away."

They said, "It would be grand!"

"If seven maids with seven mops

swept it for half a year,

Do you suppose," the Walrus said,

"That they could get it clear?"

"I doubt it," said the Carpenter,

And shed a bitter tear.

"O Oysters, come and walk with us!"

The Walrus did beseech.

"A pleasant walk, a pleasant talk,

Along the briny beach.

We cannot do with more than four,

To give a hand to each."

The eldest Oyster looked at him,

But never a word he said:

The eldest Oyster winked his eye,

And shook his heavy head—

Meaning to say he did not choose

To leave the oyster-bed.

by Lewis Carroll (1832–98)

MAKING A SPLASH

T he Marine Mammal Protection Act of 1972
protects the Pacific walrus from being hunted
in Alaskan waters, and it is currently being
considered for inclusion on the United States'
Endangered Species List. The Atlantic walrus is
categorized as a species of special concern by the
Committee on the Status of Endangered Wildlife
in Canada and is being considered for listing under
Canada's Species at Risk Act. If listed, the walrus will
be protected throughout Canadian waters. Currently,
walruses are hunted in all of their habitats, but various
governments regulate that hunting. Using traditional
tools and methods of hunting, only people native to the
Arctic regions are allowed to hunt walruses for their
meat and ivory. These massive marine creatures have
been important sources of food, oil, and hides for as long
as people have inhabited the Arctic coasts. Traditionally,
the tough hides of adult walruses were made into
flexible, waterproof coverings for skin boats, called
umiaks in the language of the Inuit, and the softer hides
of young walruses were braided into rope. Walruses'

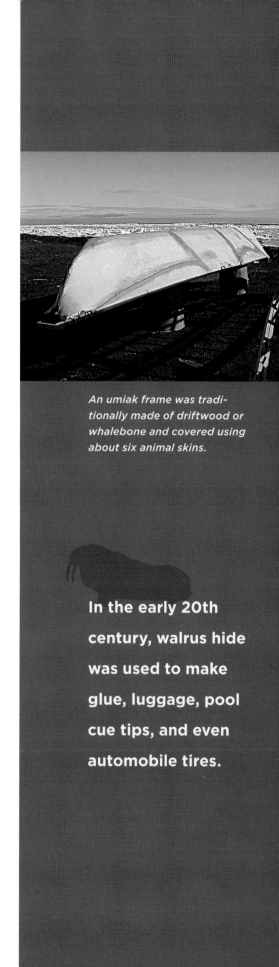

An umiak frame was tradi-
tionally made of driftwood or
whalebone and covered using
about six animal skins.

In the early 20th
century, walrus hide
was used to make
glue, luggage, pool
cue tips, and even
automobile tires.

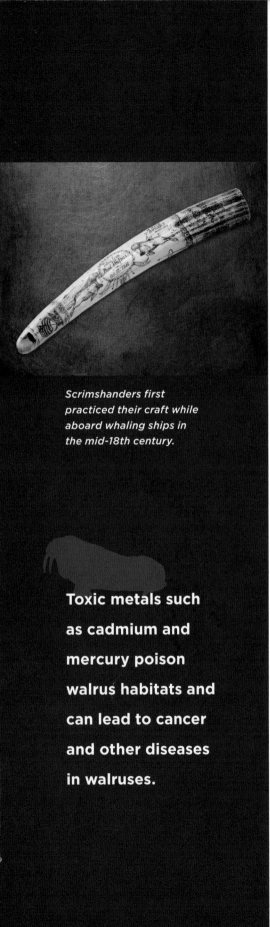

Scrimshanders first practiced their craft while aboard whaling ships in the mid-18th century.

Toxic metals such as cadmium and mercury poison walrus habitats and can lead to cancer and other diseases in walruses.

large air sacs were stretched over drums, and blubber was cooked down to make oil for lamps and cooking.

Walruses have even provided a means of entertainment. The Chukchi people of the Russian coastal regions surrounding the Chukchi and Bering seas have traditionally used walrus skin to make large, slightly stretchy blankets that are used as a type of hand-held trampoline. In a traditional game, people take turns being tossed high into the air by the others who hold the blanket taut. The goal is simple: be tossed the highest and land back on the blanket—not on the ground.

For thousands of years, Arctic peoples have valued the walrus not only for its meat and other body parts but also as a symbol of a traditional way of life. Walruses' ivory tusks have been used to make tools or weapons, such as harpoon tips, as well as artwork. The traditional art of scrimshaw involves the carving of elaborate images into walrus tusks, whalebone, and whale teeth. Only the native peoples of the Arctic are allowed to make art using body parts of walruses and whales. Much of this artwork reflects the cultural **mythology** of the indigenous peoples of the north, which has been shaped by walruses and other Arctic creatures.

The Inupiat continue to hunt walruses for their meat and blubber, which the Inupiat call koq (KOHK).

The aurora borealis was named for Aurora, the Roman goddess of dawn, and Boreas, the Greek god of the north wind.

The Inuit legend of Sedna tells how a beautiful girl was forced by her selfish father to marry Raven, who held her captive on a rocky island with no shelter and little food. Her father's guilt led him to rescue her in a kayak, but when Raven discovered the betrayal, he became angry and caused a fierce storm at sea to batter the tiny kayak. The father then threw his daughter overboard in an effort to save himself. She clung to the side of the kayak, but her father cut off her fingers, which sank to the bottom of the sea and turned into seals. Still, Sedna tried to climb aboard the kayak, but her father cut off her hands, which sank beneath the waves and turned into walruses.

Struggling to pull herself into the kayak with just her arms, Sedna begged her father to help her, but instead he cut off her arms, which sank into the sea and turned into whales. Sedna herself then sank beneath the waves and turned into a powerful goddess capable of controlling the ocean and its current. To this day, fishermen give thanks to Sedna every time they capture a seal, walrus, or whale. Pouring water into the dead creature's mouth is a sign of their gratitude for Sedna's having given up parts of herself so that the fishermen and their families may eat.

Some native peoples of Alaska and the Russian Chukchi Peninsula believe that the aurora borealis, or northern lights, contains a magical world inhabited by the souls of people who died violently. The rays of light are thought to be torches lit by the souls playing football (or soccer) with the head of a walrus.

European explorers fashioned their own myths about walruses and other sea creatures, typically portraying them as

The third floor of the historic Arctic Club building in Seattle, Washington, is lined with 27 carved walrus heads.

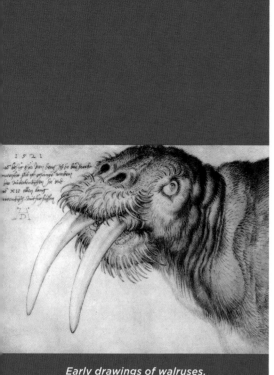

Early drawings of walruses, such as Dürer's, were often based on dead specimens or secondhand reports.

While diving, the walrus can lower its heart rate, a process called bradycardia, which helps it conserve the oxygen in its blood.

man-eating monsters. Olaus Magnus, a Swedish clergyman and explorer of the Norwegian Sea, described walruses in his 1555 book *History of the Northern Peoples* as "Great Fish as big as Elephants" that attacked humans and tore them to pieces. In 1521, German artist Albrecht Dürer created a drawing of a walrus based solely on a glimpse of a pickled walrus head that was a gift from Norwegian archbishop Erik Walkendorf to Pope Leo X. Dürer's walrus was not scientifically accurate, but it was not as ferocious-looking as many other artists' portrayals of the time. In the centuries that followed, sailors would include walruses in their folklore of the sea, describing them as unearthly and demonic.

In British writer Lewis Carroll's 1871 book *Through the Looking-Glass and What Alice Found There*, a clever walrus character appears in the poem "The Walrus and the Carpenter." Illustrator John Tenniel depicted the walrus as a fat, good-natured character wearing a jacket and floppy shoes. Nearly 100 years later, John Lennon of the British rock band the Beatles wrote the song "I Am the Walrus" for the 1967 album *Magical Mystery Tour*. The song's nonsensical lyrics have little to do with walruses, and many music critics believe the song was a tribute to Carroll's

imaginative nonsense poems, which Lennon admired.

In the U.S., walruses have typically been viewed as lumbering, comical animals. One memorable walrus character was Wally Walrus, a grumpy costar of Woody Woodpecker's in 1940s cartoons, beginning with "The Beach Nut" in 1944. Over the next 17 years, in a number of cartoons by Walter Lantz Productions, the dim-witted oaf with a Swedish accent clashed with not only Woody Woodpecker but also Chilly Willy the penguin and Andy Panda. Wally Walrus returned to cartoons in 1999 as a regular on *The New Woody Woodpecker Show.*

In Lewis Carroll's poem, the walrus and the carpenter trick a troupe of oysters into being eaten.

As global temperatures rise, chunks of ice the size of entire cities break off Arctic glaciers, reducing icy habitats.

Canada showed its regard for the walrus as a natural resource by featuring the animal on a stamp in 1954.

W alruses were once abundant in areas below the Arctic Circle; in fact, the Atlantic walrus was once found as far south as Massachusetts. Overhunting led to the disappearance of Atlantic walruses along the North American coast and in the Gulf of St. Lawrence, where they once thrived. While Pacific walruses are more numerous than their Atlantic cousins, scientists monitoring walrus populations have noted a continued decline in both subspecies. In 1931, Canada banned the hunting of walruses for **commercial** use, and the U.S. followed suit in 1941. But other countries have no hunting laws that protect walruses. Greenland, for example, continues to hunt the Atlantic walrus without regulation. Even in the U.S., Russia, and Canada, there is no limit on the number of walruses that native Arctic peoples can take. Researchers estimate that more than 10,000 walruses are killed annually in legal hunts. Many scientists believe that walrus hunting, combined with the effects of **global warming**, is no longer **sustainable** and suggest that limits should be placed on legal hunts as well.

Global climate change has been affecting ice formation

A walrus may squirt water around a deeply buried shellfish to drill it out of the sediment and then use its whiskers to grab it.

Walruses suffer the effects of exhaustion when slabs of sea ice used for resting platforms are too distantly scattered.

in the Arctic, which in turn influences walrus behavior and health. Walruses need solid ice on which to rest between periods of foraging for food. Arctic ice once remained thick and plentiful well into the summer months, but global warming and increased ocean water temperatures have contributed to faster melting rates. Research has indicated that Arctic water temperature has increased by more than six degrees in the last decade, leading to less ice for walruses, which must now sometimes travel great distances to find better conditions.

Without ice on which to rest, walruses are forced to spend more time on land, where they are more vulnerable to human disturbance and polar bear attacks. With hundreds or thousands of walruses crowded onto a rocky beach, a single disturbance can spark a stampede toward the water, leading to individuals being crushed to death. Particularly, females with young who cannot find ice away from other members of a herd may suffer the loss of calves in overcrowded conditions. In 2009, researchers found 131 young walruses dead on a beach near Icy Cape, Alaska—all had been trampled by larger walruses. That same year, in Cape Schmidt, Russia, researchers discovered that thousands of walrus calves had been crushed when tens of thousands of walruses had crowded onto a beach. Such events are now common in all walrus habitats where sea ice recedes earlier every spring.

A long-term problem that scientists foresee being a result of global warming is a depletion of walrus food sources. Global climate change is linked to increased amounts of carbon dioxide in Earth's atmosphere. As the ocean absorbs more of this chemical, the water becomes more acidic and less healthy for many marine creatures—including mollusks, which are walruses' primary food source. If changes in their **ecosystems** are too drastic, walruses may not be able to **adapt** quickly enough.

The Greenland Institute of Natural Resources and the Danish Polar Centre are studying Atlantic walruses by using **satellites** to track a number of walruses in the Labrador Sea along Greenland's coast. Each walrus has a **Global Positioning System** (GPS) device temporarily attached to its thick blubber. For several months at a time, the device sends an electronic signal that can be picked up by a weather satellite. The data that is gathered helps researchers track walrus movement—information that

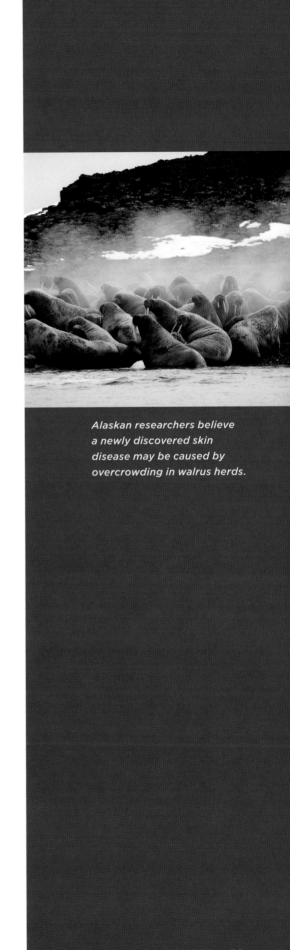

Alaskan researchers believe a newly discovered skin disease may be caused by overcrowding in walrus herds.

Younger, smaller walruses tend to stick together, foraging for food and resting together.

The Walrus Islands State Game Sanctuary off Alaska's west coast protects seven small islands where walruses gather.

may be useful in efforts to conserve Greenland's walruses.

Annually since 2004, the U.S. Geological Service (USGS) Alaska Science Center has used similar devices to track the movements and foraging behaviors of Pacific walruses in the midst of changing sea ice conditions in the summer and fall. Researchers use a crossbow to shoot the device, which is about the size of a hockey puck, into the walrus's hide. Since the hide is so thick, the device does not hurt the animal. Researchers are particularly interested in learning about the consequences of walruses spending more time on shores and beaches, especially as it may affect the **mortality rate** of calves.

Annual visual counts are made by USGS researchers, who in recent years have observed a sharp decline in the number of yearling calves. Normally, one in three females in a herd has a yearling, but in 2010, USGS walrus reseacher Tony Fischbach found that the walruses on the northwestern coast of Alaska had far fewer than that number—leading him to wonder what has been happening to the young walruses. One possible explanation was suggested in a 2004 study conducted by the Woods Hole Oceanographic Institution, which found that a number

Biologists at the Alaska Science Center get as close as they safely can to retrieve information and tag walruses.

of walrus cows were forced to leave their offspring on too-small pieces of ice while they went foraging for food. Because the mothers had to travel far, and the ice platforms were too small, the calves drowned or starved before their mothers could return.

Global warming is not walruses' only threat. Their populations are also being affected by increased human activity in their habitats. The Center for Biological Diversity (headquartered in Tucson, Arizona, with field offices in 11

Alaskan coastal water temperatures range from 31 °F (-0.5 °C) to 38 °F (3.3 °C) during the winter months.

states and Washington, D.C.) is an organization that works to protect animals and ecosystems through legal actions. The Pacific walrus has been the focus of much work by the group in recent years. One current project involves the oil industry. Despite the Marine Mammal Protection Act, which is designed to guard walruses against human harassment, oil companies in the Beaufort and Chukchi seas have been allowed to disturb walruses in those areas in favor of oil exploration and drilling. In 2011, the Center for Biological Diversity successfully sued one major oil company to block oil exploration in walrus habitat in the Beaufort Sea, but many more actions are still in progress.

Despite the challenges faced by conservationists trying to protect walruses and by researchers trying to understand walrus behavior, their projects are beginning to yield valuable results as humans witness walruses' responses to global climate change. Further analysis of this information, as well as increased public awareness of the plight of walruses, may lead to strengthened conservation efforts around the world. Pressured by circumstances, walruses need our help if they are to once again flourish in one of our planet's harshest environments.

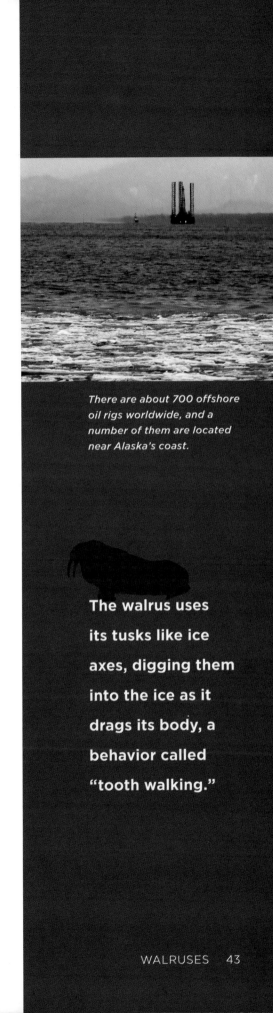

There are about 700 offshore oil rigs worldwide, and a number of them are located near Alaska's coast.

The walrus uses its tusks like ice axes, digging them into the ice as it drags its body, a behavior called "tooth walking."

ANIMAL TALE: THE WALRUS AND THE CARIBOU

The Inupiat are tied to the Arctic land and sea. These native people of northwestern Alaska and the Bering Straits region believe that all living things were created for a reason and that people and animals share a special relationship. The following Inupiat story explains how the walrus and the caribou came to be and why the Inupiat depend on these animals.

Long ago, Old Man and Old Woman began arguing over who had created the finest animals. Old Man had made the animals of the land, and Old Woman had made the animals of the sea. Old Man snatched up a polar bear and shook it before Old Woman. "See here," he thundered, "this is the finest animal in the world."

"No!" countered Old Woman, pulling a bowhead whale from the sea and waving it in front of Old Man. "This is the finest animal in the world."

Their argument grew louder and more violent, and soon all the animals fled in terror. When this happened, famine spread across the land and sea, as the people could find no animals—seals, polar bears, whales, or fish—to hunt. The people began to starve. They begged for the fight to end.

"We will have a contest," Old Man suggested. "We will each make one more animal, and we will let the people decide which is the finest."

"Agreed," said Old Woman.

Old Man gathered the people together and instructed them to judge which of the animals was the finest. He pulled a piece of fat from his bag and threw it onto the ground. From the fat grew a mighty beast with four legs, a strong body, long neck, and powerful head—the first caribou. This

caribou also had enormous ivory tusks extending from its upper jaw.

"This is indeed a fine animal," the people told Old Man.

Then Old Woman pulled a piece of fat from her bag and cast it into the sea. From the fat grew a massive creature with powerful flippers and a broad snout boasting a mat of stiff whiskers—the first walrus. This walrus had a spectacular set of antlers atop its head.

"Yes," the people told Old Woman, "this is indeed a fine animal."

The people were hungry, though, and not interested in judging a contest. Seeing this, Old Man and Old Woman told the people to hunt the animals, taste them, and then judge. So the people went hunting.

When the people tried to hunt the caribou, the animal fought back fiercely with its tusks and injured the hunters. Likewise, when the people tried to hunt the walrus, the animal used its antlers to overturn their boats, nearly drowning them.

"We cannot judge," the people told Old Man and Old Woman, "because neither of these animals is suitable."

Old Man and Old Woman suddenly felt ashamed at fighting and driving away all the animals—thus depriving the people of food. They realized that they had made a mistake. Old Man took the tusks off the caribou, and Old Woman took the antlers off the walrus. They traded, putting the antlers on the caribou and the tusks on the walrus.

"Now," the people said, "these are both the finest animals in the world."

GLOSSARY

adapt – change to improve its chances of survival in its environment

carrion – the rotting flesh of an animal

commercial – used for business and to gain a profit rather than for personal reasons

ecosystems – communities of organisms that live together in environments

gestation – the period of time it takes a baby to develop inside its mother's womb

Global Positioning System – a system of satellites, computers, and other electronic devices that work together to determine the location of objects or living things that carry a trackable device

global warming – the gradual increase in Earth's temperature that causes changes in climates, or long-term weather conditions, around the world

invertebrates – animals that lack a backbone, including shellfish, insects, and worms

mammals – warm-blooded animals that have a backbone and hair or fur, give birth to live young, and produce milk to feed their young

mortality rate – the number of deaths in a certain area or period

mythology – a collection of myths, or popular, traditional beliefs or stories that explain how something came to be or that are associated with a person or object

resistance – the slowing effect applied by one thing against another

satellites – mechanical devices launched into space; they may be designed to travel around Earth or toward other planets or the sun

sustainable – able to be renewed or kept functioning

uterus – the cavity inside a female mammal's body where offspring develop before birth

webbed – connected by a web (of skin, as in the case of webbed feet)

SELECTED BIBLIOGRAPHY

Berta, Annalisa, James L. Sumich, and Kit M. Kovacs. *Marine Mammals: Evolutionary Biology*. 2nd ed. Burlington, Mass.: Elsevier, Academic Press, 2006.

Marine Mammal Center. "The Pinnipeds: Seals, Sea Lions, and Walruses." http://www.marinemammalcenter.org/education/marine-mammal-information/pinnipeds.

Nowak, Ronald M. *Walker's Marine Mammals of the World*. Baltimore: Johns Hopkins University Press, 2003.

Perrin, William F., Bernd Wursig, and J. G. M. Thewissen, eds. *Encyclopedia of Marine Mammals*. 2nd ed. Burlington, Mass.: Elsevier, Academic Press, 2008.

Reynolds, John E., William F. Perrin, Randall R. Reeves, Suzanne Montgomery, and Timothy J. Ragen, eds. *Marine Mammal Research: Conservation beyond Crisis*. Baltimore: Johns Hopkins University Press, 2005.

Sea World. "Walrus." Animal InfoBooks. http://www.seaworld.org/animal-info/info-books/walrus/.

Without aggressive conservation efforts, some walrus populations may decline beyond the point of recovery.

INDEX